THE GARDENS OF SABA

Quran Stories for Little Hearts

by

S Khan

Goodword**kidz**

Helping you build a family of faith

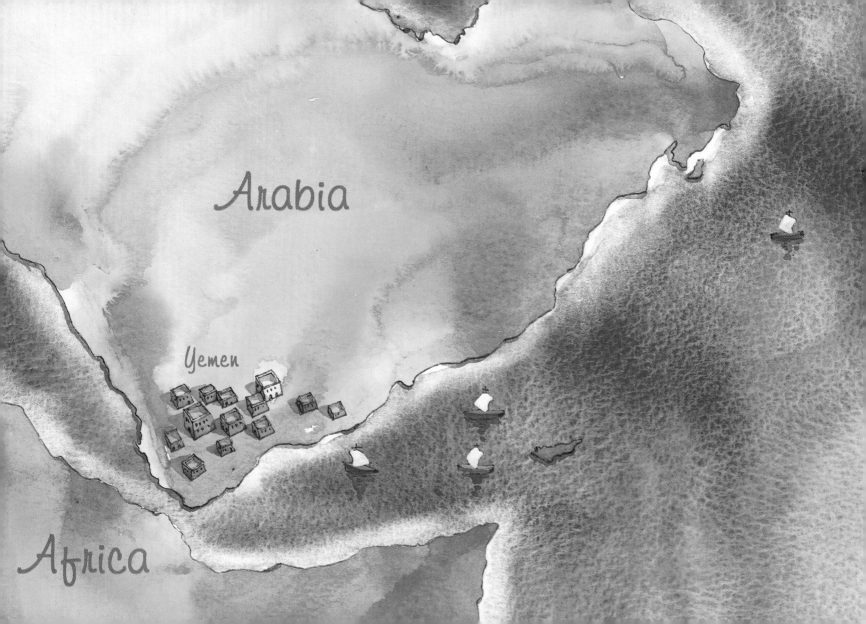

Long long ago, before the birth of the
Prophet Isa (Jesus) علیه السلام, there lived in the
ancient lands of Yemen the very rich and
powerful people of Saba, or Sheba.

The largest city of the region was Marib. For
about 1000 years the area became more
and more wealthy and reached its peak, as
the people of Saba expanded their trade
through land and sea routes.

4

6

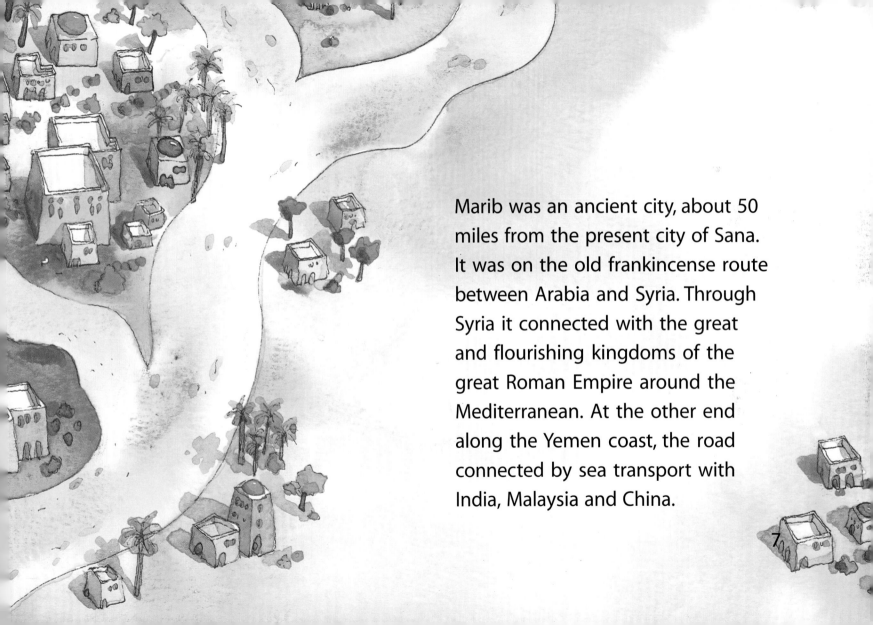

Marib was an ancient city, about 50 miles from the present city of Sana. It was on the old frankincense route between Arabia and Syria. Through Syria it connected with the great and flourishing kingdoms of the great Roman Empire around the Mediterranean. At the other end along the Yemen coast, the road connected by sea transport with India, Malaysia and China.

The people of Saba were very hard-working.
They constructed a huge dam. This dam was
called the Marib dam or *sad al-Marib*. It took
years to construct it.

8

10

The dam was about two miles long and 120 ft high. The people of Saba with their great skills made it into the best example of engineering of their times.

This dam brought great wealth to the area.
They made roads and canals. The canals were
bordered by gardens on both sides.

The trees and bushes of the lush green gardens and orchards were laden with fruits. The gardens and fields, well-watered by streams, produced a variety of fruits, spices and frankincense.

All worldly progress is achieved thanks to the help which Allah has given us. Without His blessings, we cannot achieve any success. So whenever we are successful, we should say "Thank You" to Allah for His help and remain humble and down-to-earth.

But the people of Saba, instead of being thankful to Allah, chose to become arrogant. They thought that all the progress and riches that they enjoyed were due to the clever planning of their forefathers, who so ably built the great dam of Marib. They forgot to thank Allah. They became proud and haughty.

Allah does not like arrogant people who do not thank Him. So during the seventh century A.D., when the pent-up waters of the eastern side of the Yemen highlands were collected in a high lake held back by the Dam of Marib, the wall of the dam began to crack.

18

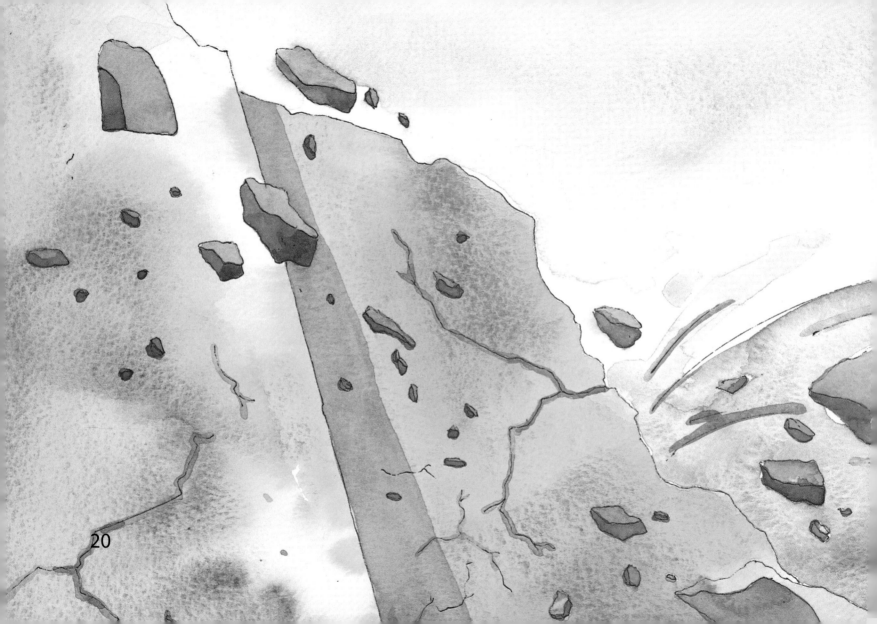

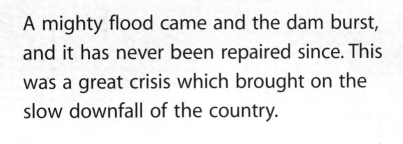

A mighty flood came and the dam burst,
and it has never been repaired since. This
was a great crisis which brought on the
slow downfall of the country.

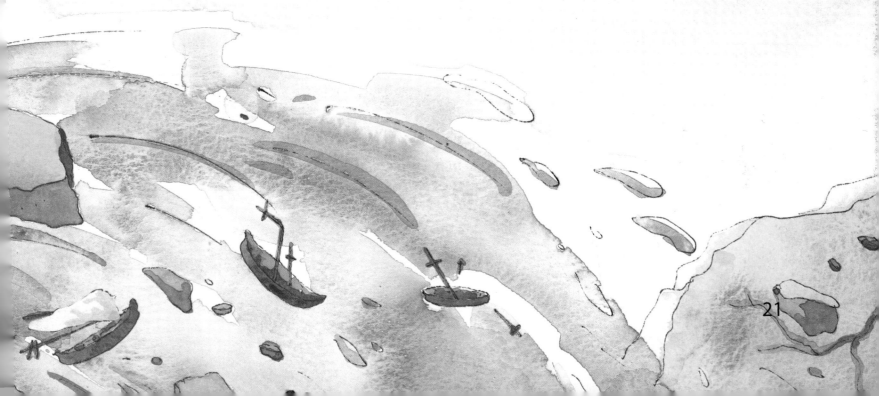

The flourishing gardens of Saba were left to turn into a waste land. The luscious fruit trees became wild, and gave place to wild plants with bitter fruit. The feathery leaved tamarisk, which is only good for twigs and wattle-work, replaced the sweet-smelling plants and flowers. Wild and stunted kinds of thorny bushes, like the wild Lote tree, which were good for neither fruit nor shade, grew in place of the pomegranates, the date palms, and the grape vines.

This punishment of the people of Saba was an example to all mankind. It reminds us that we should always be thankful to Allah for His blessings and never become arrogant and proud over our success. All success comes only with the Help of Allah.

Find Out More
To know more about the message and meaning of Allah's words, look up the following parts of the Quran which tells the story of the gardens of Saba:
Surah Saba 34:15-19